JOHN GARDNER

A SHAKESPEARE SEQUENCE

OXFORD UNIVERSITY PRESS

MUSIC DEPARTMENT WALTON STREET OXFORD OX2 6DP

This sequence was commissioned by Greenhead High School, Huddersfield, and first performed (except for No. 5) by the school choir under Neville Atkinson at the Huddersfield Town Hall on 3 December 1964.

The percussion parts are optional and transferable. The full battery consists of glockenspiel, xylophone, triangle, tambourine, sleigh-bells, tabor, side-drum, bass-drum, cymbals, and gong. As many of these as are available may be included in the instrumentation.

It is not recommended that the work be performed with piano solo accompaniment, here included for purposes of rehearsal only.

Full scores and percussion parts are available on hire. Piano duet players play from the full score.

Duration 15 minutes

SECULAR

SSAA, piano duet,
and optional percussion

OXFORD

A Shakespeare Sequence

John Gardner

MUSIC DEPARTMENT

OXFORD
UNIVERSITY PRESS

A SHAKESPEARE SEQUENCE

JOHN GARDNER
(Op. 66)

For Neville Atkinson

1 IT WAS A LOVER AND HIS LASS

 Printed in Great Britain
OXFORD UNIVERSITY PRESS, MUSIC DEPARTMENT, WALTON STREET, OXFORD OX2 6DP

For James Iliff

2 WHO IS SILVIA?

A
B
SOP. 1
p legato sempre
Who is Sil - vi-a? What is
SOP. 2
p legato sempre
Who is Sil - vi-a? What is
ALTO
p legato sempre
Who is Sil - vi-a? What is
staccato sempre
Senza Ped.

she? That all our swains com - mend her? Ho-ly, fair, and wise is
she? That all our swains com-mend her? Ho-ly, fair, and wise is
she? That all our swains com - mend her? Ho-ly, fair, and wise is

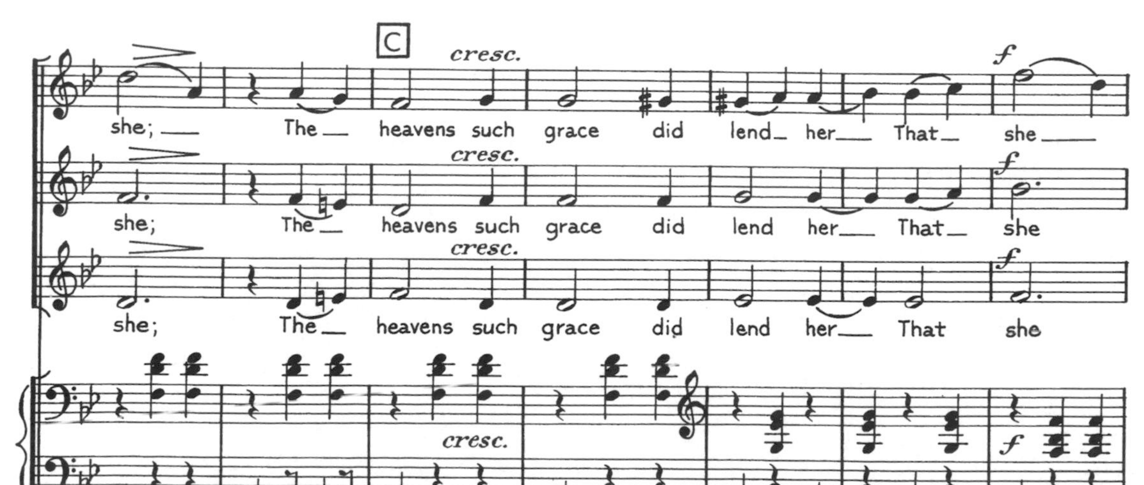
C
cresc.
f
she; The heavens such grace did lend her That she
she; The heavens such grace did lend her That she
she; The heavens such grace did lend her That she
cresc.
f

D
p
might ad - mir - ed ___ be.
p
might ad - mir - ed ___ be.
p
might ad - mir - ed ___ be.
mf
dim.

E
p
Is she kind as ___ she is fair? For beau - ty lives with kind - ness:
p
Is she kind as ___ she is fair? For beau - ty lives with kind - ness:
p
Is she kind as ___ she is fair? For beau - ty lives with kind - ness:
p

F
cresc.
Love doth to her eyes re - pair, ___ To ___ help him of his
cresc.
Love doth to her eyes re - pair, ___ To ___ help him of his
cresc.
Love doth to her eyes re - pair, ___ To help him of his
cresc.

G
f
blind – ness, And, be – ing helped, in – hab – its there.
blind - ness, And, be - ing helped, in - hab - its there.
blind - ness, And, be - ing helped, in - hab - its there.

SOP. 1
SOP. 2
ALTO 1
ALTO 2
H
p
mp
cresc.
Then to Sil - vi - a let us sing, That
Then to Sil - vi - a let us sing, That
Then to Sil - vi - a let us sing, That
Then to Sil - vi - a let us sing, That
mf

f
Sil - vi - a is ex - cel - ling, Then to Sil - vi - a let us sing,
Sil - vi - a is ex - cel - ling, Then to Sil - vi - a let us sing,
Sil - vi - a is ex - cel - ling, Then to Sil - vi - a let us sing,
Sil - vi - a is ex - cel - ling, Then to Sil - vi - a let us sing,

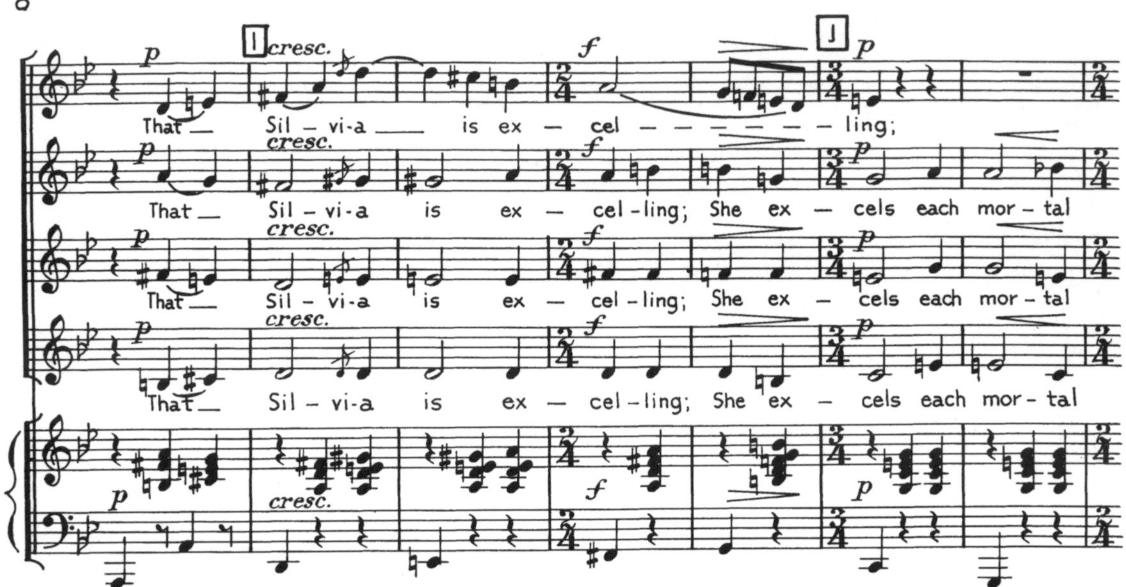
I
J
p
cresc.
f
That — Sil – vi-a — is ex – cel – – – – – – – ling;
That — Sil-vi-a is ex – cel-ling; She ex – cels each mor – tal
That — Sil – vi-a is ex – cel-ling; She ex – cels each mor – tal
That — Sil – vi-a is ex – cel-ling; She ex – cels each mor-tal

K
L
cresc.
ff
p
Up – on the dull earth dwell – ing: — To — her —
thing — Up – – on the dull earth dwell – ing: To — her
thing Up – – on the dull earth dwell – ing: To her
thing Up – – on the dull earth dwell – ing: To her

let us gar – lands bring, To her let us gar – – – – lands
let us gar – lands bring, To her let us gar – – – – lands
let us gar – lands bring, To her let us gar – – – – lands
let us gar – lands bring, To her let us gar – – – – lands

3 O MISTRESS MINE

cresc.
B
f
— and hear! your true love's com — ing, That — can sing both high and low; —
(Tutti)
p
cresc.
— Trip no fur – ther, pret - ty sweet — ing, Jour - neys end in lov - ers meet -
f
C
— — ing, Ev – 'ry wise — man's son doth — know.
p
(Solo ad lib.)
f
p
What — is love?
cresc.
f
p
D
cresc.
'tis not here-aft — — — er; Pre — — sent mirth hath pre – sent laugh -
cresc.

p
cresc.
mf
E
(Tutti)
p
— — ter, What's — to come is still un - sure: In de - lay — there
p
cresc.
mf
p

cresc.
lies no plen — ty; Then come kiss_ me,— sweet and twen — ty!
cresc.

f
Youth's a stuff will_ not en — — dure.
p
f
mf
dim.
pp

For Tony Arnell

4 IF MUSIC BE THE FOOD OF LOVE, PLAY ON

𝅗𝅥 = 60
p
cresc.
Con Ped.
A
SOP.
p
cresc.
If mu — sic be the food of
ALTO
p
cresc.
If mu — sic be the
f
dim.
p
cresc.

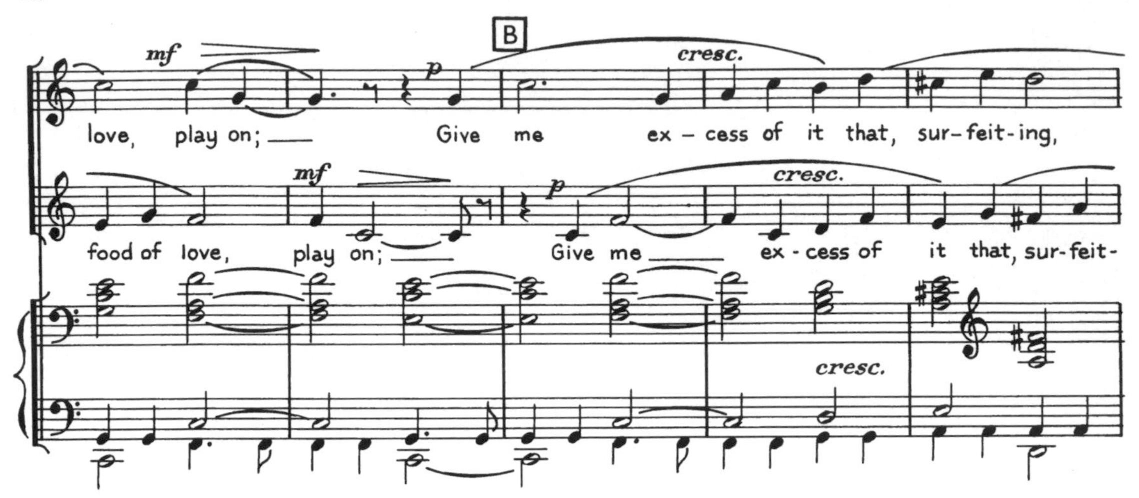
B
mf
p
cresc.
love, play on; — Give me ex – cess of it that, sur–feit–ing,
mf
p
cresc.
food of love, play on; — Give me — ex-cess of it that, sur-feit-
cresc.

C
f
dim.
p
The ap – pe – tite may sick-en, and so die, — and so die. —
f
dim.
p
-ing, The ap — pe-tite may sick-en, and so die, and — so die. —
f
dim.
p

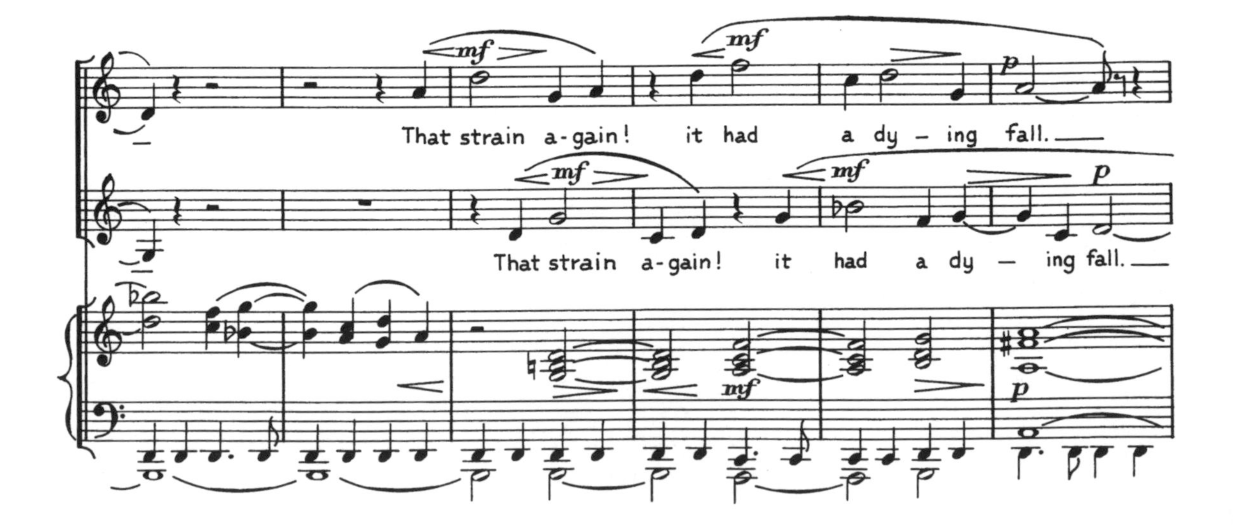
mf
mf
p
That strain a-gain! it had a dy – ing fall. —
mf
mf
p
That strain a-gain! it had a dy – ing fall. —
mf
p

D
f
O! it came o'er my ear like the sweet sound That breathes_ up-on a
O! it came o'er my ear like the sweet sound That breathes up-

E
dim.
p
mp
mf
bank of vi — o-lets,_ Steal — — — ing and giv — — ing o —
-on a bank of vi — o-lets,— Steal — — — ing and giv — — ing

F
pp
rall.
a tempo
p
— dour. E-nough!_
o — — dour. E-

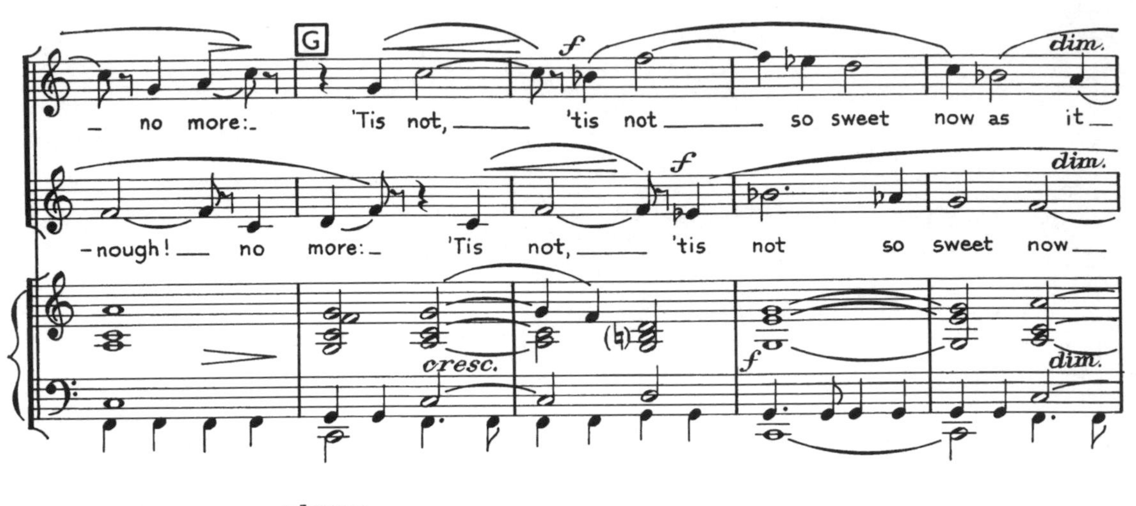
G
f
dim.
— no more:— 'Tis not, —— 'tis not —— so sweet now as it —
f
dim.
-nough! — no more:— 'Tis not, —— 'tis not so sweet now —
cresc.
f
dim.

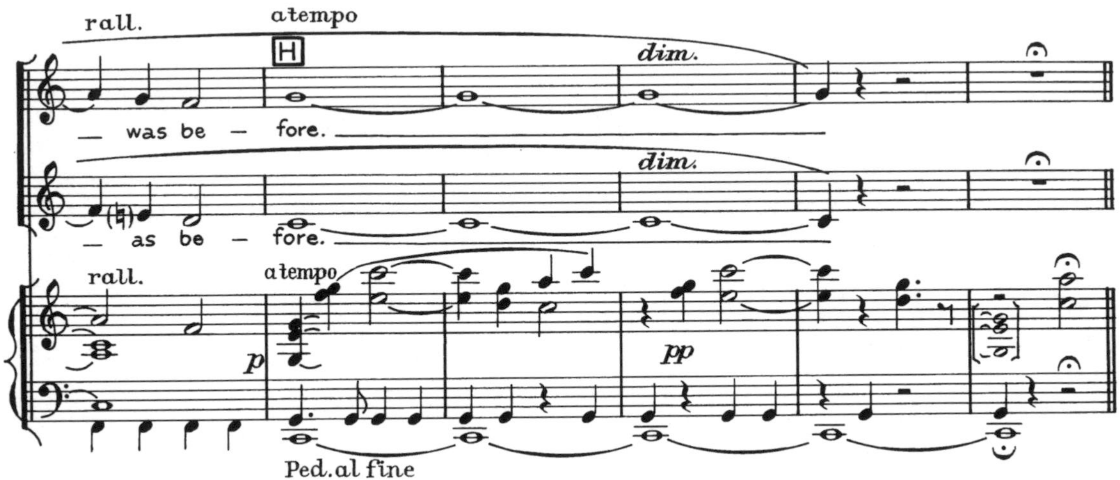
rall.
a tempo
H
dim.
— was be — fore. ——
dim.
— as be — fore. ——
rall.
a tempo
p
pp
Ped. al fine

For Andrew Byrne

5 TAKE, O TAKE THOSE LIPS AWAY

♩ = 96

A

SOP. 1

p

Take, O take —

SOP. 2

p

Take, O take —

ALTO

p

Take, O — take —

p mp mf dim. pp

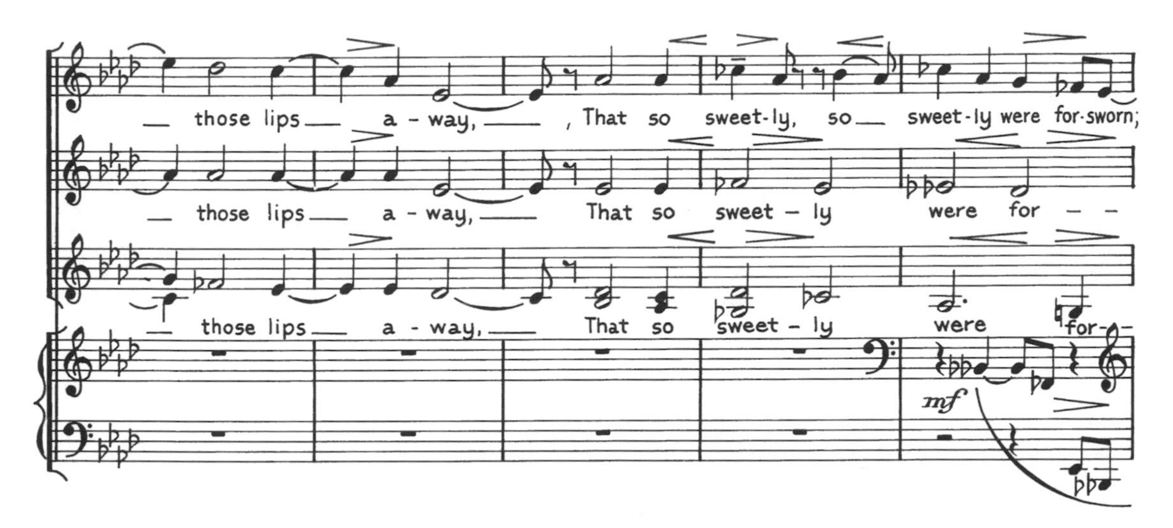
those lips a-way, , That so sweet-ly, so sweet-ly were for-sworn;
those lips a-way, That so sweet-ly were for
those lips a-way, That so sweet-ly were for-
mf

B
And those eyes, the break of day, Lights
-sworn; And those eyes, the break of day, Lights
-sworn; And those eyes, the break of day, Lights
p cresc.
p cresc.
mf
p
mf
marc.
Senza Ped.

C
that do mis-lead the morn: But my kiss-es bring a-gain,
that do mis-lead the morn: But my kiss-es bring a-gain,
that do mis-lead the morn: But my kiss-es bring a-gain,
mf
p
cresc.
p cresc.

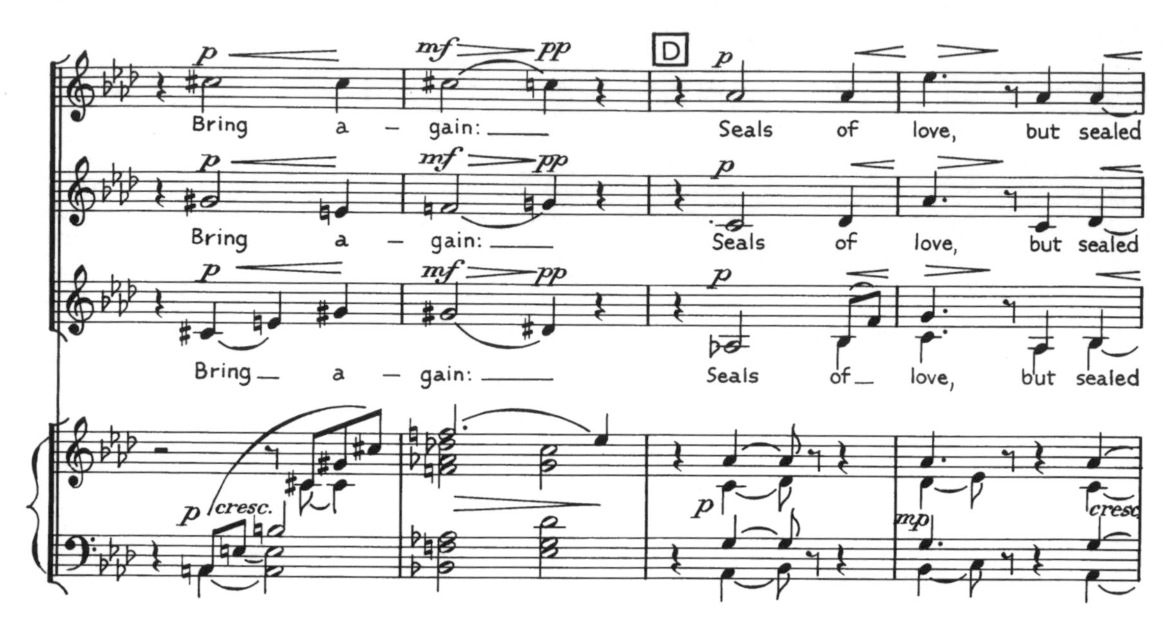
D
p mf pp p
Bring a – gain: Seals of love, but sealed
Bring a – gain: Seals of love, but sealed
Bring a – gain: Seals of love, but sealed
p cresc.
mp
cresc

E
f p mf p
in vain, Sealed in vain!
in vain, Sealed in vain!
in vain, Sealed in vain!
f
pp

p
mp
ppp
Ped.
*

For Alan Collingridge

6 FULL FATHOM FIVE

♪ = 148
Tutti or semi-chorus in unison
p
Full fa-thom five thy fa- ther lies, Of his_ bones are
p

A
mf
p
co - ral made; _ Those are pearls_ that were his eyes: No-thing_ of him
mf
p

cresc.
that doth fade, But doth suf-fer a sea - change In - to some-thing rich_ and
cresc.

B
ff
strange.
ff
dim.

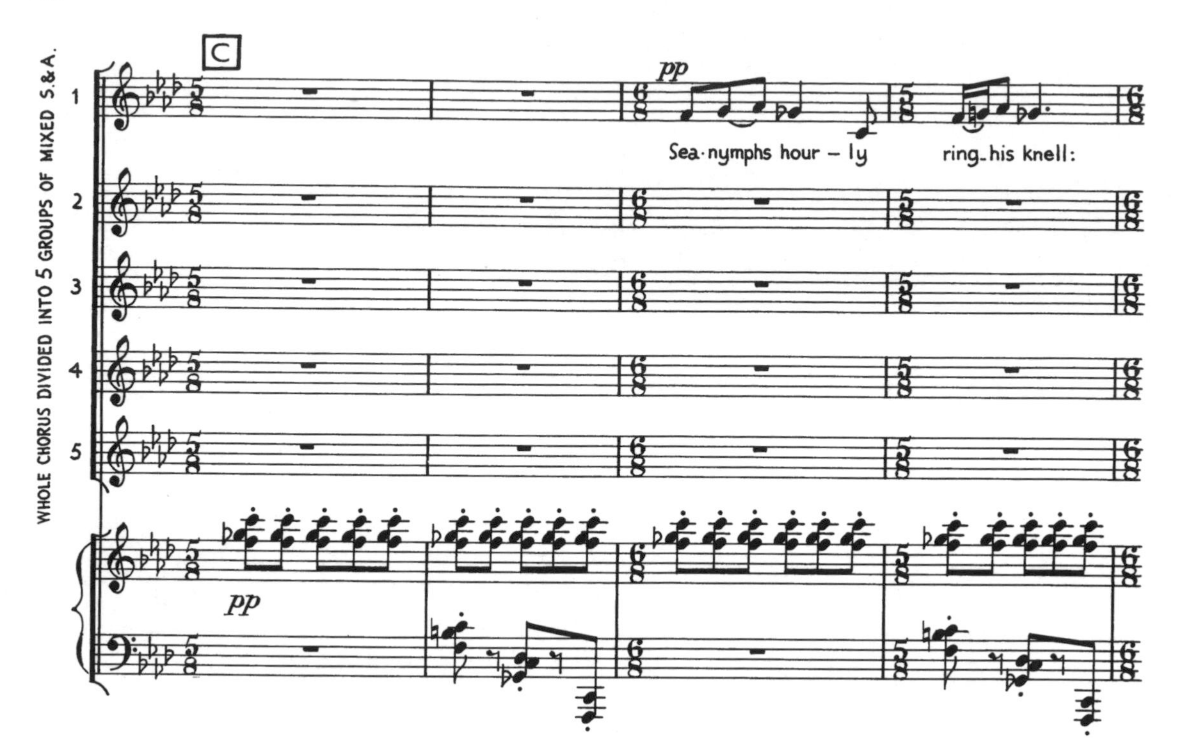
C
WHOLE CHORUS DIVIDED INTO 5 GROUPS OF MIXED S.&A.
pp
Sea-nymphs hour - ly ring_his knell:
pp

D
p
"Ding - dong, ding - dong."
mf
Hark! now I hear them: "Ding-dong, bell, —
p
Sea-nymphs hour - ly ring_his knell:
mf
"Ding - dong, ding - dong."
mf
Sea-nymphs hour - ly ring_his knell:
cresc. poco a poco

E
1
2
3
4
5
f
ff
ding – dong, ding – dong, bell."
Hark! now I hear them: "Ding-dong, bell, ding – dong, ding – dong,
"Ding – dong, ding – dong." Hark! now I hear them: "Ding-dong, bell,
Sea-nymphs hourly ring his knell: "Ding – dong, ding – dong."
Sea-nymphs hour – ly ring his knell:

F
1
2
3
4
5
f
bell."
ding – dong, ding – dong, bell."
Hark! now I hear them: "Ding-dong, bell, ding – dong, ding – dong,
"Ding – dong, ding – dong." Hark! now I hear them: "Ding-dong, bell,

G
1
2
3
4
5
mf
p
bell."
dim. poco a poco
ding - dong, ding - dong, bell."
mf
dim. poco a poco

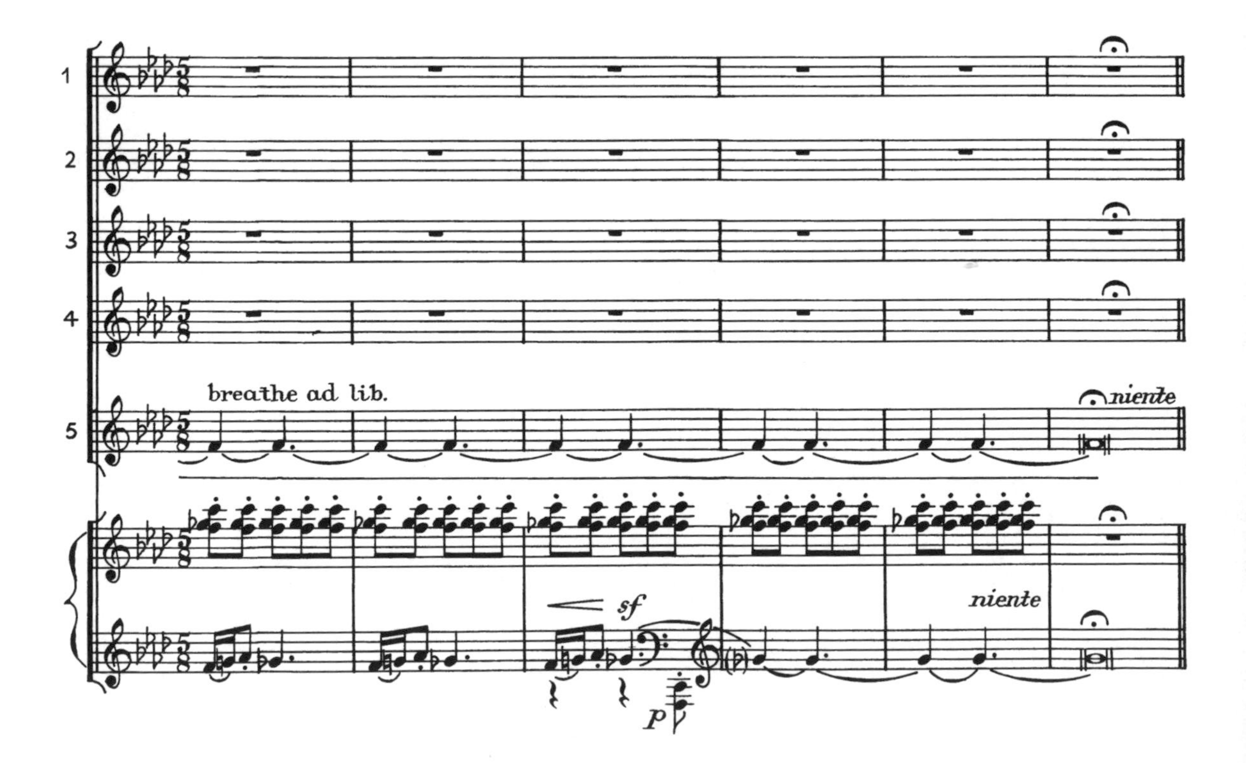
1
2
3
4
5
breathe ad lib.
niente
sf
p
niente

For Ronald Vincent Smith

7 ORPHEUS WITH HIS LUTE

* Solo sings upper notes throughout.

D
cresc.
flowers E — — — ver sprung; as sun
Ped. * Ped. * Ped. * Ped. *
f
p
— and showers There had made a last – ing
cresc.
f
p
Ped. * Ped. * Ped. * Ped. *
E
p
Spring. Ev' – ry – thing that
Ped. * Ped. * Ped. * Ped.
cresc.
heard him play, E — — ven the bil – lows of the sea
cresc.
* Ped. * Ped. * Ped. * Ped. *

F
G
ff
mf
Hung their heads, and then lay by.
Ped.

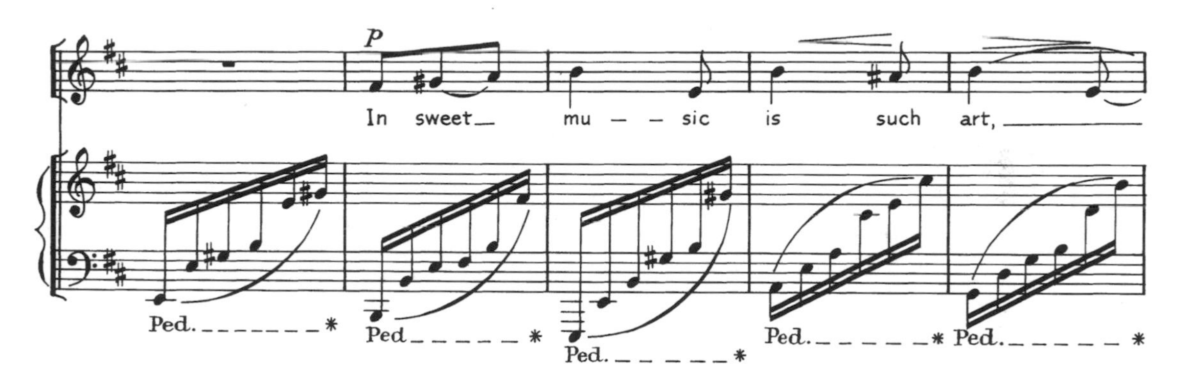
p
In sweet mu - - sic is such art,
Ped.

H
mf
dim.
p
Kill - ing care and grief of heart Fall a - sleep, or,
Ped.

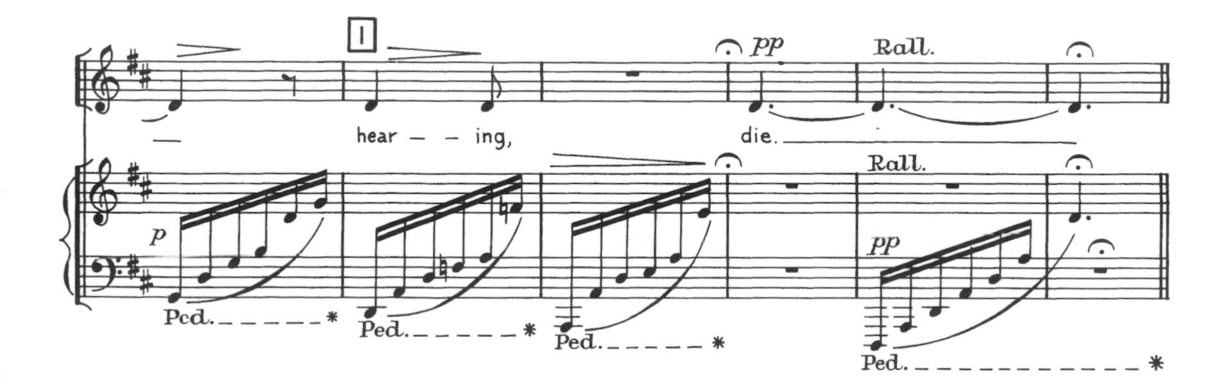
I
pp
Rall.
p
hear - - ing, die.
Ped.

For Emily Jane Pullein Gardner

8 UNDER THE GREENWOOD TREE

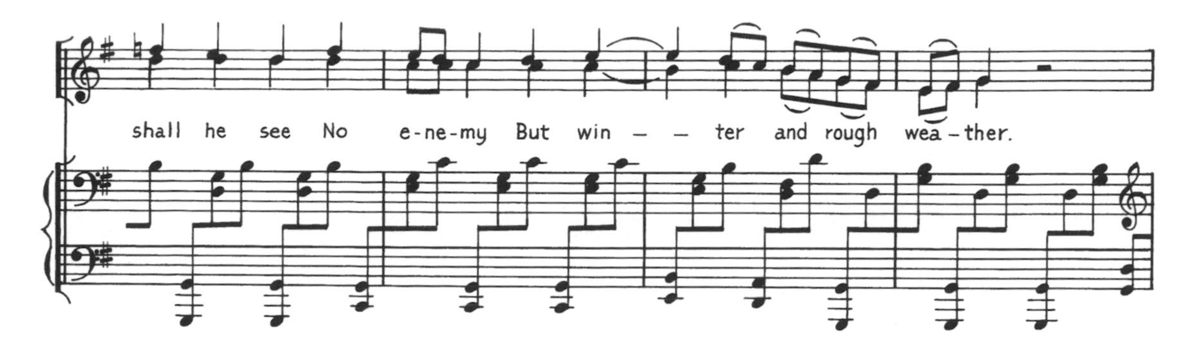
shall he see No e-ne-my But win — — ter and rough wea-ther.

CHOIR 2 S & A
C
p
Who doth am-bi-tion
p

shun — And loves to live i' the sun, — Seek — — ing the food he

D
eats, seek-ing the food he eats, And pleased with what he gets, — Come

hi – ther, come hi – ther, come hi – ther, come hi – ther ! Here shall he see No

en-e-my But win — — ter and rough wea – ther.

E
cresc.
f
p cresc.

F
CHOIR 1
ff
Un – der the green-wood tree — Who
CHOIR 2
ff
Who doth am – bi – tion
ff

1
loves to lie with me, And turn his mer-ry note, and turn his
2
shun, And loves to live i' the sun Seek-ing the food he eats, seek-
1
mer-ry note Un-to the sweet bird's throat, Come hi-ther, come
2
-ing the food he eats, And pleased with what he gets, Come hi-ther,
G
1
hi-ther, come hi-ther, come hi-ther! Here shall he see No en-e-my But win-
S
come hi-ther, come hi-ther, come hi-ther! Here shall he see No en-e-
2
A
come hi-ther, come hi-ther, come hi-ther! Here shall he see No en-e-

H
1
S
2
A
— ter and rough wea-ther, wea – ther, wea – ther,
-my But rough— wea-ther, wea – ther, wea – ther,
-my But rough— wea-ther, wea – ther, wea – ther,

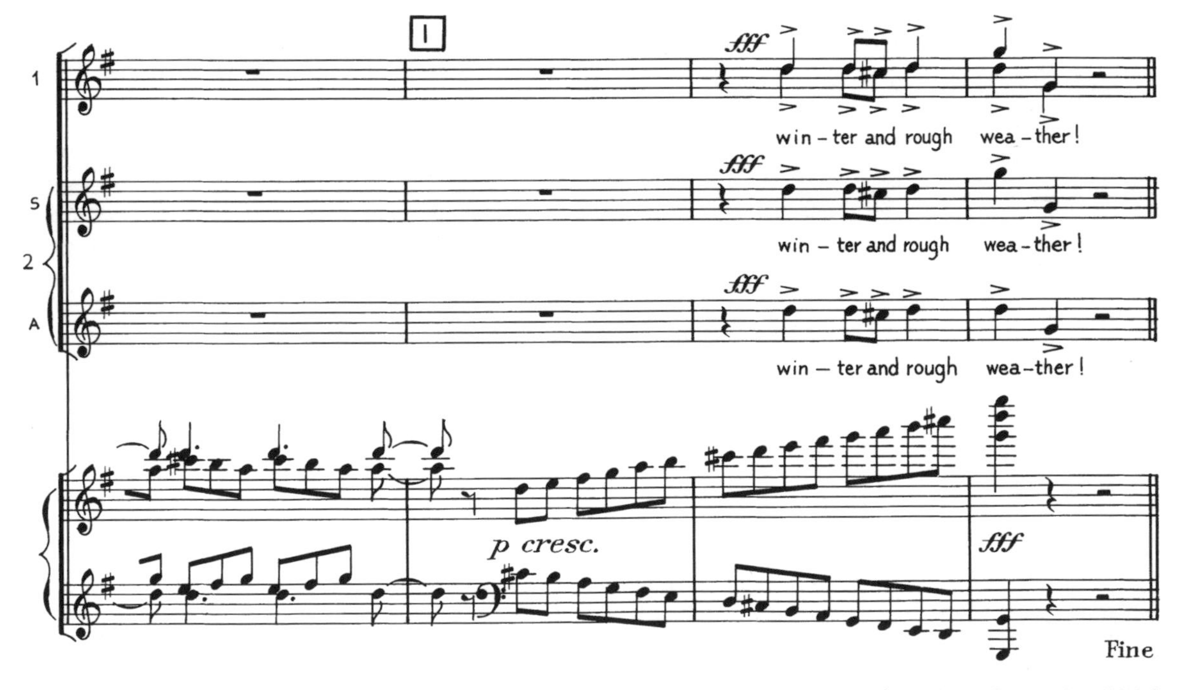
I
1
S
2
A
fff
win – ter and rough wea – ther!
win – ter and rough wea – ther!
win – ter and rough wea-ther!
p cresc.
fff
Fine

New Malden, Summer 1964, No 5 added December 1964

Halstan & Co. Ltd., Amersham, Bucks., England

OXFORD UNIVERSITY PRESS

A Shakespeare Sequence GARDNER
OXFORD
UNIVERSITY PRESS
www.oup.com
ISBN 978-0-19-341191-3
9 780193 411913